Epicurean Ecstasy

More Poems About Food, Drink, Herbs & Spices

Epicurean Ecstasy

More Poems About Food, Drink, Herbs & Spices

Cynthia Gallaher

A Publication of The Poetry Box®

Editing & Book Design by Shawn Aveningo Sanders.
Cover Design by Robert R. Sanders.

ISBN: 978-1-948461-17-7
Library of Congress PCN: 2018954642
Printed in the United States of America.

Published by The Poetry Box®, 2018
  under The Poetry Box Select imprint
Beaverton, Oregon
ThePoetryBox.com

Seize life! Eat bread with gusto, Drink wine with a robust heart. Oh yes— God takes pleasure in your pleasure!

— Ecclesiastes 9:7

Contents

Found Champagne Poem in an Unclaimed Wisconsin Corner

51-degree Champagne at the 42nd parallel,
you pull a magnum from the plastic pail ice bucket,

foil and wire cage tossed aside,
to grasp the cork between thumb and forefinger,

then turn the bottle.
Pop. Sizzle. Stars.

liquid plays flute
as I pour blanc de noirs for both of us

seated in our
folding chairs.

shall we toast?
to what, today?

Napoleon Bonaparte said of Champagne,
"In victory, one deserves it.

In defeat, one needs it."
though it's a day of neither defeat nor victory,

but part of some other scaffolded demolition or
yet ungrouted building block

toward something
we yet don't understand.

the Champagne happily chips away
at it a little

the way its grapes chip
at chalky hillsides northeast of Paris for nourishment,

to later be crushed
and create bottlesfull fermented and aged.

yes, I found this poem
like we found this special bottle

marked down in the corner bin
of the dusty liquor store.

and now at our card table outdoors
we breathe hillside air

and swallow tiny bubbles
of carbon dioxide.

am I, like you say, this half-hour's mermaid of the Extra Brut ether,
or you, my midnight prince of prestige cuvée,

or merely both as simple as this Tuesday sparrow-song night,
yet still savvy enough to quote Dorothy Parker?

"Three be the things I shall never attain:
envy, content and sufficient Champagne."

Egg World

which came first, the chicken
or an earth either oval or round?

which wobbles like a raw egg
or spins like a cooked one?

taking the same time as an over-easy whirl,
adding orderly, odd moments to peck around

and get cozy on her nest,
the chicken lays her egg.

I open coop roof
to gather one.

I see a face, a suggestion
for sustenance for brain, nerves, eyes,

for those in shades of white and shades of brown.
I see protein for a planet.

the shell, a seamless earth,
the egg white, its foamy, wavy waters.

yolk at the core, the blazing fire,
and between shell and substance, an airy atmosphere,

a place to catch my breath between crescent bites,
amid revolutions and rotations

in synch with the moon,
which stays in synch with the egg,

keeps in time with the chicken,
marking the hour we continue to see sunrise

encased among straw each morning,
right in time for breakfast.

Generations of Beans

"I was determined to know beans."
— Henry David Thoreau, *Walden*

after my widowed mother married a civil servant,
meat and mashed potatoes again graced our table.

she whispered to me, "only the poor eat beans,"
yet we stored dried beans in our cellar, just in case.

those beans sometimes did duty on picnic bingo cards,
was what danced beneath accountants' fingers,

and enemies' boasts didn't amount to a hill of.
they're what I glued, along with

red lentils, green dried peas, onto black
construction paper and oatmeal boxes in school.

my tongue forgot the cooked variety's taste,
but a 20-something trip 900 miles south

lavished mouth's memory by means of
Cajun red beans' spicy punch on Rue Royale.

after wedding bells back north, I also heard my macro-Mexican
husband call our shower gift of potato masher – a bean smasher!

used when pintos swell deep pink and plump, only to give up under
pressure, turn creamy and fragrant under the soupy sway of garlic,

onion, cilantro, cumin, all air-biscuit free with epazote,
a velvety fold with brown rice into corn tortillas,

and like mom, I store beans in basement cellar,
but also in cupboard's jars, to add to savory simmerings.

she visits, sees our humble kitchen,
but doesn't know our hidden grand prosperities

in great northern, black turtle,
cannellino, toscanello.

Template for Tempeh

"The culture that binds the beans together
binds the people as well."
— Scott Tibbott

clothing's woven, food can be, too,
with patterns crafted in Java's underground,
earth's finely carded fiber, planted with seeds,

handed off to the sun,
to twist, turn, spin water and soil's richness into yellow,
black and red soybean bobbins.

post-major harvest, modest steam,
nature lends a shuttlecock push,
weaves soybeans into mushroomy tempeh mats.

two thousand years ago, through matchmaking skills
of Indonesian crafters: the friendliest of molds
and heartiest of soybeans met and married.

loom set, gregarious mold casts its social network over
and through a tray of soybeans, warping and wefting
into fermented whole.

it's not fake meat, but real tempeh,
bean-shaped cobblestones deliciously close,
mortared in edible white.

thickly gessoed canvas absorbs splashes of tamari,
flavors of ginger, garlic, chili pepper,
and according to the whim of the chef, becomes sculpture

cubes sautéed, rectangles grilled or grated slivers steamed,
each breadth, a healthy hive, an ongoing agreement
that agrees with you more than other soy,

fritters away its own enzymatic woes,
and would even chew for you if it could,
but then you'd miss out yourself.

Yogurt: Another Pearl of Great Price

if the world is your oyster
then yogurt is your cultured pearl,
tangy white roundness,
polished protector.

brilliance to the eye
or health to bones
can start out as
one, big irritation.

single grains of sand
press sharply faceted shoulders into oysters,
while savvy upstarts place a zealous foot or two
in the milk supply door.

in spite of the odds,
pearls and altruistic
probiotics
prevail.

some Young Turk who slung a goatskin of warm milk
across a camel's back, took it on a wild ride under sun's glow,
never thought trail's end would reveal
our first cultured food.

since then, we've strung luscious pots
of the stuff
around the globe
like a benevolent, living necklace.

All-American Blueberries

Great Spirit, as always, creative,
plucked blueberries from outer space, say the native,
leaving tiny bright holes in each place,
to let bees beam them down, into bowls.

stardust waxy bloom disappears in your hands,
and there loom berries, fully dressed,
in dark navy microfiber, pressed
beneath lacy underpinning.

was it from the beginning,
that blueberries yearned to be
the rock-and-roll, rococo fruit,
one that zigs and zags in tastes.

flavors of sweet noon
at midnight,
coolness of twilight at dawn,
dual worlds encased.

these silent sapphire islands are known to float
in tumultuous seas of whipped cream,
and hover like umlauts
to accent tossed salads, supreme.

hold counsel throughout the pemmican-eating nation,
bespeak what makes dried buffalo keep,
between its own blue streaks
of preservation.

from Orac to the Omega,
from Maine to Michigan, it's by this,
we lengthen our years, among deeply hued spheres
of blueberry bliss.

Here Come the Strawberries

low-down strawberry plants play their cards
close to modestly woven chests,
every hand, making sure to keep
the queen of hearts hidden.

they hide quite a few,
where girlish pulses
become rhythmic womanly beats,
as mothers beget daughters.

a rosy network
where veins and arteries
connect, form full-blooded bodies,
ready for suitors.

block-long rows, virginally bedecked in May white,
where bees swoon among papery, invitational blossoms,
transform into succulent Valentines
riddled with sexy sienna seed messages.

each berry becomes June's most beautiful bride,
languid and scarlet on a unmade bed of straw
even before betrothal, once plucked, tasty celebrations
last for weeks at the farmers' market.

you may have missed the wedding,
but now gladly attend the reception,
as the vendor hands you a woven basket
filled with ripe, firm strawberries

tumbling toward you
like oversized ruby engagement rings,
it is you
who catches the bouquet.

Massachusetts Cranberries

afloat, a party of redheads on a giant waterbed,
squeezed into cozy corners before they freeze
by sleepy workers hip-high in prophylactic waders.

or are they gathered like scarlet colonies
of miniature planet mars vanquished to earth,
set loose from ancient-armored spaceships barrels.

through the processing factory window
brigades of tangy spheres bounce madly
florid against the backdrop of thick snow.

then bagged like pachinko parlor booty,
to soon become Thanksgiving sauce,
tart juice tender to holding tanks,

or strung white, red, white, red,
both self-contained and exploded on thread
in rows with popcorn.

Harvesting Goji Berries

pluck one off the vine,
but dare damage.

such delicacy needs coaxing

with wind as if from pursed lips, or an in-person
journey to its dance floor of branches

to shake and shimmy a request,

hereby winning a basket of the happiest berries,
each laughing from a petite core,

dusky pink marquis diamonds,

with tastes of tea, tomato and raw almond,
or perhaps of what lingers just after

a kiss with a stranger.

you smile, stay balanced, gojis loosen and fall.
how many others have done themselves in

for something so small.

Figs: Animal, Vegetable *and* Mineral?

is trans-species hanky panky taking place
in plain sight, open air, beneath fig leaves?

pushy, stingless, pollen-ridden wasps
lose wings and antennae on one-way trips

through fig's valve-like eye
to burrow in its fertile maw,

to weave wispy wasp feet
into fleshy furnishings,

line walls thickly in onyx,
strew carpets with amethyst pillows.

to help become the food that
separates the civilized from barbarian,

yet make fools of those
who savor figs as a strictly vegan treat.

Pomegranate: Tree of Knowledge, Tree of Life?

was this the real apple
of Eden's eye?
tempting as it flashed
a rubied crown
from its shrubby tree?

from generations of orchards,
we've hand-plucked possible worlds,
seeded unlikely stories,
even gave Persephone fuel
to keep one foot out of the grave.

standing now on God's green earth,
can we be happy? pick one.
bite one. take a chance.
we, no longer standing in a garden
stained crimson with fresh sin.

or do old ways continue
to play themselves out
in pathological disorder?
can mere math and myth triumph?
Jews count 613 bloody pomegranate seeds

to mirror numbered laws, all but broken,
while beneath pomegranate's
leather hide beat
glistening, garnet hearts,
convened.

unique,
no close relatives,
in a genus by itself,
and through its wholeness,
we cross chambers,

glimpse a paradise we can't see,
unless opened from inside.

Beat of the Pumpkin Drum

big orange, Illinois,
rotund autumnal
heartland center,

pumpkin territory.

August's thrum begins to drum
against tough hides
of pumpkin acres,

the ripening signal.

tiniest ones line window sills
along back porch halls,
while grandest usher

Cinderella on route to the ball.

the beat continues through harvest time,
as burners heat for packing plant's
canning extravaganza,

on behalf of la calabaza.

raza rise from the south,
close to pumpkin's native birthplace,
up to its new home north, factory rat race,

with 10 weeks of good wages in the bargain.

heat and jargon turn up pressure gauges,
the beat rages
over 12-hour days, seven a week,

pumpkin gold catches its fall winning streak.

men and women line up

for cleanin', slicin', sortin'
up here in Morton, Illinois,

not a mecca of salt,

but perhaps sweat and tears,
where workers keep returning
after 10 and 20 years.

they've even built a church around it
in old Soledad,
with money from

la calabaza, el norte and God.

by November, raza again heads south to Mexico,
the Morton factory turns quiet,
while throughout the USA, another riot,

as cans of pumpkin fly off grocery shelves.

creamy, cooked and canned,
the forefront of another Thanksgiving,
lending America a hand,

to make a pie, then get on with real living.

it's the grand finale course in West Virginia,
Washington, Wyoming, with ample room for
another slice of pumpkin pie, then back to video games,

hour-long naps and sinks full of smeared-up dishes.

how is it that no one asks or wishes
to know where pumpkins start out
or who brought them to the end of the line.

please pass the wine.

after the last empty can's discarded
and final hunk of pie digested,

the workers will still be fully vested,

with another hefty slice of cash,

for their annual 10-week drill,
when the autumn beat
resumes

in Morton, Ill.

Multi-taskin' Watermelon

what do you bring to a rock festival?
sleeping bag? check.
cans of soup? check.
box of matches? check.
watermelon as canteen?

my arms too full to check.

walk through rock fest gates,
skinny legs wrapped in fatigues,
tank-topped, flat-bellied,
still a virgin, but pregnant
with desire

for rock-and-roll.

watermelon as chair holds me
as I await Amboy Dukes and Ravi Shankar
with 60,000 others in Stevens Point,
10,000 more than Monterey Pop
but only a tenth the supreme get-together

attracted the year before at Woodstock.

two rocks, round as squashes
straddle kindling and dried weeds,
which I light, set atop with open can of soup
balanced like a dancer
on stone feet,

bon appetit!

I sleep with watermelon under my knees
so no one will steal it,
meanwhile, strolling hippie dudes
choose 2 am to storm the pup tent,
not for watermelon,

but its payload of four lasses, sleeping shoulder to shoulder.

I use watermelon as weapon,
roll melon and me forward,
kick one dude in the jaw
with my foot,
while a fellow sleep-interrupted pal

knees another through canvas curtain.

the sorrowful stragglies
keep a 20-foot distance
the rest of the weekend,
shaking their heads.
One calls from afar,

"where the heck do girls like you come from, anyway?"

I hold the watermelon
over my head with two hands.
"we grow the likes of us in pods like this, man,"
I say, hurl the watermelon
on the ground in front of me,

splitting it into four pieces

dudes jump back
farther still,
my tent mates kneel,
dip and dine
on cool sweetness,

red liquid dripping down our faces.

Doesn't a Cut Apple Look Like a Pair of Lungs?

aflower this year, right after,
not before, the last frost
in April,

drawing in honeybees
or "white man's flies,"
the Native Americans called them,

to pollinate among
pink and white blossoms
as quick as sneezes.

fruits of the rose family,
inhaling, exhaling, enlarging,
through the hot summer

'til a buxom bouquet
wafts heavy
on the limbs,

your woody stems,
pipelines
to your roots,

big-winded apples
breathe a sigh of relief
come September.

pippin, piñata, pomona,
pomme, a poem,
you have each become one.

nourished and woven
by the breeze,
airy and juice to the bite,

so appealing
so cider-friendly
so honeyed and crisp

if you loosen and fall
into a tub of water
under your own leafy shade

you won't get the wind
knocked out of you
or belly flop,

but buoyant
and bobbing,
you float.

Pruning Grapevines

did wild grapevines goad humanity
to tame them, their vines profuse, prolific,
trekking recklessly cross-terrain,
unabashed in tangling with
and choking botanic competitors.

winding upward, stealing sunlight from
treetops, to lay seed drunkenly
in their Dionysian orgies,
to drop fruits in quantity, not quality,
as they crawled away on mornings after.

who first applied the discipline
of the knife, the mathematics
of trimmed canes, numbered buds,
leaf-to-fruit ratios,

the cutting back, tying and spacing
to unwind the chaos of Medusa
on a bad-hair day
into shorn tendrils dressed with ribbons.

who watered, unshaded these leafy canopies
that hung over once minute fruits
to now swell with sun and engorge clustered globes
with juices that thrill human tastebuds.

it's an ancient war story, a battle to this day,
fought as wild grapevines advance
to face every spring with a pruning,
a forced retreat at the hands of humans,
xylem vine fluid weeping from cut wounds.

here in the vineyard, generations reside
together in each vine, trunks may mark 80 years,
with great-grandchildren newborn shoots
spreading controlled fecundity of this year's cultured grapes.

finally, all may seem at peace
with this new domestication,
thousands of grape families
now settled and fenced among human ones,
all for mouthfeel, aroma, release and escape
of wildness itself bottled in vines' fermented wine.

but would grapevines, if you let them,
reach down into their primitive urges,
unleash from these vineyard wires,
knock aside anything in their way,
set out in all directions, harkening
to the wanderlust intrinsic in their vines.

Cherries vs. Cherry Blossoms

every bite into a cherry
creates a wound
a risk of hitting the pit too hard
a moment over too soon.

I let cherry juice
run down my face,
it feels so ancient Rome
to imagine blood
should taste like tart cherry juice
instead of its metallic saltiness.

is this why the Japanese write
about cherry blossoms
so prolifically
instead of cherries themselves?

is there something too dark
about what's consumed,
what's been ravished by bees,
what we deface with our hunger
and bruise with our teeth?
cherry blossoms
bloom for just a few days,
a time of transience when Japanese gather
for hanami, spring blossom-viewing parties.

"The most exquisite cherry blossom trees
bear no cherries," say the Japanese.

these sakura, temporary beauties,
we leave untouched, except for our sight, smell,
and pen, enjoyment from afar,
as if each were a star.

*Sakura: cherry blossoms

If Earth Were an Orange

*In New Zealand, a giant squid was found
with eyes the size of oranges, the largest eyes on earth.*

if earth were an orange,
it would stare up at a strawberry moon,
reflecting light from the sun, a hot air balloon.

and we, backyard gardeners
or connoisseurs sniffing corks,
would appear to merely vibrate

like charmed quarks.

Chocolate and Cocoa: Valentines Crafted 3,000 Years Ago

before this dark treasure was converted into Swiss truffles,
cocoa began as Mayan food of the gods,
before it was served on European holidays
as foil-wrapped Easter rabbits, candy Santas,
Valentine hearts and Hanukkah coins,

it was xocolatl, bitter water from
ground cacao beans,
imbibed in private by Mexican leaders
who drank 30 cups a day
mixed with hot chili peppers, vanilla and corn.

3,000 years post discovery,
chocolate coats the globe
in a luscious genealogy
that even museums trace
to draw Sunday crowds.

the promised tastes of finely milled
bars and bonbons, tickling more
than tastebuds, are celebrated like a rap star
at spas that offer cocoa massages
and mocha facials.

using good fat to overwhelm bad,
there's a new twist to the notion of
"take two aspirin and call me in the morning,"
calling instead for two daily squares
of the deep, dark variety,

making sexy meltdown in your mouth,
teetering on the impossibly possible brink
of being the closest thing we have to a legal opiate,
with lounges streetside instead of dens in back alleys,
contraband in every purse, a love lift,

with new willingness to woo ourselves
and seduce our hearts into health.

Are Kisses Sweeter Than Tupelo Honey?

beehives, heavy with resplendent summer,
hang honey from myriad roofs of the comb.

in this subdivision of golden-walled houses,
pollen-laden residents
and groundskeepers dressed
like Kendo masters,
dance around sweetness
and one another.

pre-hive to palaces of sweetness,
its workers carted by truck,
lugged to these farms
like so many prisoners in stripes,
not locked up
but limited by fertile radii
of flight paths,
to stick close, to pollinate
cantaloupe vines, lemon trees, buckwheat, almonds,
apples, onions, broccoli, avocado
and carrot crops.

every honey hive's 12,000 angels of agriculture
hum in C-sharp below middle C,
each devotee devoting an entire lifetime
to turn out 1/12 of a teaspoon
of nuanced lavender flower or orange blossom,
transforming pre-digested nectar in wax cells
into nature's perfect food,
a recipe field-tested for 10 million years
freshly cured by the fanning of wings.

Ginger's East Meets West
and Back Again

crossing yet another longitudinal border,
ginger's medicinal and culinary power pen
redraws maps and silhouettes of cultures.

to Asians, it's half of everything, to westerners,
a gastronomic plaything, taking on the toy-like
guise of gingerbread storybook shapes.

each level teaspoon starts somewhere as rhizome,
looking more like misshapen sock monkeys
than curvy hips of svelte Ginger from Gilligan's Island.

she who warmed and sweetened innards of TV viewers
in ways only Thai food could decades later. Ever since,
legions of cruise ship goers on 3-hour tours and beyond,

never leave shore without ginger's capsules
or a pirate's patch of essence on their arms
to ward off seasickness.

will time reveal more about this pungent spice
as we grate further into juicy lands of white ginger,
its healing and tasty havens as mysterious as Shangri-La.

Oregano Has Left the Restaurant

smells like Canale's Pizzeria
on Chicago's northwest side

where minty, oily, nose-tickling
aromas of oregano once hovered,

along with odd-named members
of the real "Pink Ladies" girl gang,

Tootie, Zorine and Twitch,

pizza in the 1950s was big news,
maybe bigger than Elvis,

oregano? not so much,
but after more than a half-century,

its covert ways as antidote
for food poisoning, parasites

now grow. who'd know?
this era when antibiotics reach,

grapple, then throw hands up
in surrender to bacterial resisters.

no match for the green-panted upstart
who can start a rumble

with e. coli, salmonella, candida,
trichomonas, even high school warts!

showing the toughest crowd that oregano's
even more powerful than the loaded revolver

old man Canale kept behind his pizza counter.

Peppermint Hello

we held the deed,
but it might have taken over.

we didn't know it was in the
backyard when we bought the house.

it lay low, dried & small
at our Halloween arrival,

but we found its siblings'
peppery party aroma

and tongue tingle among
our striped Christmas candies

while the plant itself
slept under snow,

waiting until spring
to whorl out of ground again,

point at us
with prolific saw-toothed leaves,

residence taken in the shadowed corner
at the foot of the deck,

there, when the other family moved out
there, to give us an ancient Greek greeting,

holding out its fragrant sprigs
as a friendly welcome.

we have wandered here and there,
mobile of foot and through modern propulsion,

as I'm writing this poem in Vermont, for one,
not in my Illinois home.

but peppermint is perennial,
you can count on it to be there,

yet it's not beyond spreading
through your yard, and your neighbors'.

we put up gray lattice,
to rest its veiny leaves, firm shoots,

and pop
its purplish greenness.

we thin it out each year,
but not too much,

and once in a while
we invite some top deck

to add a bite of tangy coolness
to a cask of sun tea,

or grassy pungency
to Persian rice.

we coexist nicely together
in our urban Midwest homestead

we give it space,
within flawed human reason,

and it gives us
a kindly kick to the nose

every time we crumble
a leaf in hand.

Green Tea's Ceremony Within

it's the Asian paradox,
modern, stressed Japanese
seeking refuge in old ways.

some gather in boardrooms
and sip what millennia ago
was brewed from a handful of leaves

blown by accident
into the emperor's
hot water kettle.

the way of tea has had its way,
amidst Coca-Cola signs, raging trucks
and the clatter of multi-million

heels hitting concrete instead
of stockinged feet shuffling
inside a garden-side teahouse.

a tea ceremony of the heart takes a deep bow
through each cup imbibed in downtown Tokyo,
to express principles of

harmony, respect, purity, tranquility,
as well as nourish with phytonutrients,
protect with antioxidants, oxidize fat.

another late night under bright lights,
but the tongue tastes tea on hillside forest
on a rainy afternoon, its own chartreuse umbrella.

later, in the mad crush of subway passengers,
the tea drinker's still virtually seated on a tatami,
to admire a seasonal scroll, listen to the fire,

smell incense mixed with aromas
of freshly whisked matcha,
live life in spite of one's wabi-sabi urban self.

Cool Beans

shade-grown coffee
shields me from the sun

even giant coffee beans
won't stunt my growth

its daily grind protects me
from my regular foibles

enriching me
in aroma, antioxidants,

benchmarking my weight goal to match
a sack of its unroasted beans – 60 kilos.

there's something sweet in coffee's bitterness,
a bright morning in its darkness.

this Ethiopian bean splits
a double-sided headiness

and offers ultimate sips
toward intelligence, concentration,

and as for conversation, it's sister to gardenia's
star-like blossoms forming a snowy belt

between tropics of Cancer and Capricorn,
in fruition,

caffeinated sky watchers
stay awake past midnight

to see constellations
even to sunrise

that place in time
where a fresh pot is surely waiting.

Chamomile Earns Its Wings

babies' first herb, polka-dotty chamomile
sings its yellow-crowned lullabies, offers
a pillow filled with down-curled petals.

its pale tea warms in a bottle, sits close by
to calm colic, align new little teeth
with moon's orbits,

holds baby's hand
and strokes downy hair
until he falls asleep.

manzanilla to the Tex-Mexicans,
"little apple" of fruity aroma,
the finest weave fragrant curtain blanket.

using hand-plaited innocence to un-jangle nerves,
even non-tea drinkers listen as chamomile's mom
urges, "c'mon, it can't hurt!"

yet when served in a beer stein,
this healer among flowertops is powerful enough
to set a grown man back on his feet.

golden angel chamomile plays nicely
with other herbs, shows impeccable manners,
provides good example like an elder sister,

creeps on the ground with a safe, satisfying,
never-rude attitude, but if trampled underfoot,
only grows more prolific,

but never pushy, its sweet, ample disposition
unwittingly nudges you to health if you let it,
one cupful or dusky-pollened petal at a time.

May You Have Salty Days Ahead

to sit in the heavily wooded Appalachians,
it's hard to imagine remnants of Iapetus Ocean

300 feet beneath us,
filled with 600 million year-old brine,

saturated juice of amniotic fluid,
blood plasma, lymphatic circulation,

starter liquid of worldwide
nation states,

the sea-like soup we swim in,
mineral springs from which we stir.

historically, too little of it,
now too much, a modern profusion.

"restricting salt is about as easy
as cutting back on blinking," one M.D. said.

yet ancients' lack thereof
often meant annihilation.

again reaching the outskirts
of civilized life sometime in the future,

might salt be worth more than books or gold?
we raise gardens, we butcher meat,

we tap water from the deep,
but without salt from far-flung locales

would life as we know it, change,
starting with the gentle stanch of salty kisses?

would we mourn the Cyprus black of pyramid shapes

the Galos salt caves of Krakow,

the Celtic grey of Irish seas
launching unseen fireworks in our mouths,

the Egyptian knack for preserving mummies,
the Mexican offerings at the ofrenda,

rites of purification,
disintegration of the dead,

the kosher coarseness of migrations,
Himalayan reds drawn from loftiest rocks,

fleur de sel caviar, salt flowers raked from
great sheets along Atlantic shores,

floating like snowflakes,
smelling of violets.

the easy preservations of olives, cheese,
salami, anchovies, and brining of American turkeys.

could our millennial blood hold steady
at 0.9% salt, dissolving our

fatigue and cranky moods, dancing with water
as a balanced path to rehydration.

oh crystalline structure of
sodium and chloride,

cheap and positively charged,
iconic ions we take for granted,

to be valued at any price
next time we lack.

let's relish the pinch, the dash,
between thumb and forefinger

the half-teaspoon's disappearing
act in boiling water,

the salt grinder's mild cascade
across a platter of vegetables.

sprinkle it lightly through
your days on earth, but may you sprinkle it,

seeding life's highs as well as lows,
where watermelon can become sweeter,
tears more savory.

Broccoli Transplantation

when did I wind my way out of
childhood's bitter broccoli forests

cease after-dinner hours alone
at the formica table, engulfed in shadows

of overcooked, stunted trees,
picking through branches and trunks

with an uneven fork?

at what level of green did broccoli
become estate landscaping,

colorful curb appeal next to
grilled snapper & quinoa,

play host to sesame seed,
olive oil drizzle

and fresh lemon, each new guest
condiment clinging to this urbane veggie

sending floodlights of
acquired flavor to new heights.

Season's First Crop: Asparagus

wild asparagus served on snow,
spears surrender to my frosty blade,
soon stand at attention
in fridge's half-full drinking glass.

thin as chartreuse, spring, kelp,
moss and sap green
colored pencils in the mason jar
at my desk.

does size matter for a vegetable
renowned for its aphrodisiac qualities,
and can grow
s e v e n inches in one day?

i've been in a long engagement
with my garden, waited three years
to steam, serve and spread
these vernal shoots with butter.

no matter if you wash them down
with fine French wine
or water from
the backyard hand pump,

you'll provide a heady "asparagus pee"
on your next latrine visit,
but only if blessed with
the DNA to savor its grassy fragrance.

Do I Hear a Bell Pepper?

even a sharp knife can't wedge
between snappy cayenne and biting jalapeno
deliciously heated arguments.

meanwhile cool cousin, bell pepper,
blows in bouncy from the dampened garden,
ready to ring in occasions of sweetness.

to lend watery crunches,
lively elocutions
to dinner greens, luncheon tuna.

in September's rows, peek under
leafy windows to find a United Nations
of peppers in session.

white, green, red, yellow, orange,
purple, brown, black,
a coalition of culinary diplomats,

to support compendiums of food,
not to represent their own interests,
but be bowl for seasoned beef,

rice and cheese, when stuffed,
and if not enough,
carry savory spreads and dips

to lips as crudité spoons,
add multi-winks of brilliant hue
to otherwise ordinary stew.

The Irish Potato Famine

it was a long tumble for the humble
potato, to roll its way
from Andes mountains of Peru
to Western Ireland's rocky hills.

as much of a journey from west to east
as the Irish themselves had made,
wandering the opposite
east to west.

from India,
through Europe,
to this little island
in the middle of nowhere.

a place for the Celts of old, Irish of the new to rest and
mind their own business for a few beats of history,
to teeter on the edge of the world
with nowhere left to go but the ocean.

how dare they embrace this green verdant island
to grow fresh food and surround themselves
with ocean waters lavish with fish,
some said.

who were the Irish to laugh and crack jokes,
play music, sing and dance a jig,
and trade what extras they had with neighbors
who filled the minuses they lacked in return.

as if there weren't
a whole world out there to conquer,
a market and new industrial system to uphold,
others agreed.

and so the Irish were forced
to hold back their native tongue,

and let others' nets
fish their shores.

to give up their land,
to grow wheat, barley and oats
for others far away,
whose faces they would never see.

entire Irish families squeezed
onto small poor garden plots,
to raise the only food they could keep,
and still owe rent, that wasn't cheap.

that's when the potato arrived on the scene,
starchy, nutritious, of plain expression,
a South American transplant
not knowing where it was.

but generously rooting itself,
growing to bulk up
enough of its kind in just one acre
to feed a family of 10 for a year.

the Irish came to depend on potatoes
as other cultures do bread,
and while most cannot live on bread alone,
the Irish thrived on potatoes

for breakfast, lunch and dinner, lunch, dinner
and breakfast, and dinner, breakfast and lunch,
and that's a bunch,
of potatoes.

the potato grew as the most favored food
of the Irish from west to east,
until one day, nearly overnight,
a strange mist rolled in from the waters

bringing a spotted disease, a potato blight,
ruining crop after crop

from the east
to the west.

and where there once were potatoes,
now there were not,
and the ones they dug up
were nothing but rot.

there were no more potatoes
for breakfast, lunch or dinner,
and the Irish peasants
grew thinner and thinner.

while the wheat and the barley
and the oats and the fish
kept ending up nicely
in another's dish.

and the Irish, who long teetered on the edge of the world,
teetered on the edge of death,
and in order to live and have something to give,
they took a hard look west.

and those among them who didn't die
somehow made it across the sea,
it's the story of my ancestors
that's been handed down to me.

Sweet Potatoes: Garnets in the Rough

pointy witches' noses,
stray hags' whiskers,
mud encrusted
as farmers' gloves.

sweet potatoes and yams
line Vicksburg bins
unglamorously
as sleeping sows.

we lug them, reluctantly,
like clots of dirt into stainless kitchens
as Thanksgiving icons
of scarcer times.

what some think
garbed like the village idiot
on the outside,
God has granted gold internal wisdom.

cut open, a fall bonfire flames,
lighting lanterns of buttery bliss
to carry radiance through winter months,
without can or carton.

old as history, slow to digest,
powerhouse of vegetables,
when buffalo could not be felled,
when corn failed, the answer

lie at everyone's feet,
though one might have to
dig a little
ways down.

Roots: Dense Treasure

underground vegetables
of the first chakra, muladhara,
the rootedness we imitate in yogic poses,
grounding down in order to expand upward.

oh, dirt dwellers who absorb soil's richness:
carrots, parsnips, white and sweet potatoes,
beets, radishes, rutabagas,
turnips, sunchokes,

onions, shallots, garlic,
celeriac, yams, yucca,
kohlrobi, ginger, turmeric,
jicama, horseradish, daikon.

opposite of the burial we give compost,
instead we unearth these powerhouses,
dense treasures of minerals,
but unlike iron ore or emeralds,
bauxite or bloodstone,
galena or garnets,

that are crafted into tools atop workbenches
or faceted to accompany marriage proposals,
such rocks won't meet
our primal sustenance,

as do these sub-surface healers, tough survivalists,
self-preppers to aid and abet deep appetites
through hearty stews, roasted medleys of singed colors,
warm and spicy purees that stick to our bones

and balance our root chakra
beyond winter.

Tomato Inheritance

heirloom DNA weaves an asymmetrical
carpet of zaftig tomatoes,

fostering awe and enough
to feed our urban neighborhood.

Cherokee Purple, Mortgage Lifter, Brandywine,
Green Zebra, Moneymaker.

streaky hearts, the occasional gossamer
wing, others toned and ripped

with earthy tendon and muscle,
big easys to grow, hard to vanquish,

even when the gardener works two commuter jobs
between backyards of neglect and unpredictable weather.

soon, a paper bag brigade, as back fence
friendly as we who nurture the contents,

share odd cuttings, dried seeds,
soup, sauce and pickle recipes.

our stovetops grow splattered as butchers' aprons,
and cupboards bear sealed radiance.

how much science goes into splicing
vines as obedient-as-bow-ties,

hydroponic grainy, brainy cousins,
uniformly shaped, eye-popping and glossy

in the grocery aisle. still, lackluster performers
between sheets of salad dressing

and primeval tastebuds used to what's riper, redder, realer.

Humble Onion

small eternities, new stories, each year form
circuitous plots, underground dramas
in toasted vermilion, reed yellow, dusty white.

they arise every summer in backyards,
shed filmy skins as if from burnt shoulders,
someone always forgetting the sunscreen.

utterly ordinary
on a cutting board, each onion honors
its fate to kitchen knife.

count each layer a heartache, strife,
parallel universes to your own tight nervous tangles,
release valves to mature palate's tastes and tempers,

willing to put away childish shun-onion ways,
to move bravely toward fajitas,
French soup, onion tarts.

later, lessons to slice them root to stem
instead of clean across,
chill hemispheres in the freezer,

as you chop other vegetables
waiting in the wings,
in order to save your tears,

the way the years
have trained you
to do the same.

Sesame and Flaxseed Fandango

on toe shoes shaped like sesame seeds,
the ballet dancer performs a series of relevés,
then spins her shoes into tahini.

tahini pushes between clean, bare toes,
to the envy and applause of hummus,
halvah and baba ghanoush.

meanwhile, flaxseed spills as prolifically
as Niagara Falls from stage
to orchestra pit.

the tuba gets clogged,
but there's not a dry eye
in the house.

flaxseed oils lubricate complexions,
eyes, bones and joints of audience members
dressed head to toe in linen,

as well as dancers in
umber and ochre
tulle.

throughout the theater
high heels, oxfords, mary janes
and loafers,

become pestles
to the mortar of earthy, nutty
choreography.

Sprouts

is the tangled tango at the salad bar
a dance floor? or ritual of mung, alfalfa,

garbanzo, radish sprouts,
at the superfoods temple.

skinny legs genuflect
as regularly as altar boys.

how many times have your hosts dried,
died and arisen from pure water?

no clock, climate, soil or sunshine,
only moisture needs coax you to unwind

your wiry explosions of life to jette
in a roundabout way.

little born again
beans and seeds

find ultimate, elysian fate
on my plate, in one batch,

doing jelly-armed jigs
as they go down the hatch.

Holiday Hours Alongside Walnut Bowl

winter sets in, walnuts arrive.

nutcrackers pass around bowlfuls,
conversations swim.

inside each heady shell, its
double-lobe concepts

thinks it is, thus knows it is,
need it repeat?

or are walnuts abstract
butterflies that flit above surfaces,

skirt edges of bookshelves
without censure or review.

we, holiday philosophers at leisure,
sit and spar, feed cortices, lift spirits,

crack walnuts and knuckles
together on this fireside sofa,

see how deeply we can dive before
scraping nut-littered floor.

before falling deliciously, deeply,
into year-end hibernation.

Brown Rice Life Coaches

hardheaded little buddhas
rise from legs that fail to roam,
feet wrapped in wet chartreuse
of terraced paddies.

wading workers are the ones
to dance clockwise and counter around
shoots, who dip and whip
arms to harvest and thresh.

small brown crowns
take bows along the road
to macrobiotics' "big life,"
where little bones build larger ones,

the skeletal structure of diet number seven,
cups of green tea
for breakfast, afternoon snack,
then brown rice for lunch and dinner,

for a solid week.
to some,
to eat is
to eat rice.

what can you do in 45 minutes?
teach a class before the bell rings,
get to Broadway if you live 45 minutes
from Broadway.

swim 100 lengths of the pool at a steady clip,
and cook brown rice in between,
grain domesticated millennia ago
to suit both today's multi-taskers

or those who count each measured spoonful as meditation.

Oats: The Last Grain

when cool, misty hands
passed over wheat and barley fields,
a few stray oats pushed up a "V" for victory
waving at farmers, as if to say, "What about us?"

taking them for weeds,
farmers took them down
but slowly noticed oat had a grain of its own,
perhaps of meager use in the stalls or henhouse.

if the last becomes first,
how come oats ended up
in the equine's feedbag
instead of on the king's table?

with knight-like strength, able to battle
cold climates in its husky unarmed coats,
encourage poor soil to bring out its inherent richness,
and carrying a legacy, oats transfers fortitude

to whomever consumes it.
would it be out of line to say
it was missed back in 1816,
when a shortage left thousands of horses starved

and a pony-powered system lie outmoded for a season,
to lead someone to give transportation a new spin
with steedless steads, bicycles, followed by motor cars,
then a world too soon dependent on speed,

a whirl slowed only amid spiraling lipid
and blood sugar levels, and a realization
that oats aren't only for horses,
nor are they weeds.

The Birth of Whole Grain Bread

venus on a half-size cutting board,
effigy of knead,
she rises from a slough of yeast,
miniature clouds cascade with bubbles,
chase stormy flecks of bran and germ.

venus becomes still life,
loafing in my oven,
warm and giving
she falls from her pan,
but not from our graces.

between her pauses and special places,
is what defines fresh, fragrant bread,
where butter or olive oil rush hungrily,
like waves to shore.

Simply Alfalfa

might frugal poets' square meals end
where fodder of champion horses
and lowly cows begins?

Arabs called alfalfa "father of all foods,"
but is his progeny limited to barns
instead of around kitchen tables?

are today's limp iceberg salads, greasy fries,
oversweetened catsup – our preferred fare
from what's considered trough feed?

or could father alfalfa lead us,
like children, back to
lavish green's simple path?

as sage in intent as in color,
dime-a-dozen capsules of alfalfa
lie forgotten in junk drawer corners,

common as bottle caps,
yet each its own tray of vitamins,
cabinet of minerals.

wholesale, bargain-table
wound healer, blood and body purifier,
who can discount you?

elite doctors beg more lucrative answers,
while masses invite you to
their rough-hewn tables.

Insides and Outs of Popcorn

behold the unpopped harvests
from not-quite-popular,
quasi-crafty, semi-shabby
Midwestern places: Ridgway, Illinois,
Valparaiso, Indiana,
Marion, Ohio, Hamburg, Iowa.
zea mays everta! popcorn!

claiming ancestral home
in old New Mexican bat caves,
serving as elder shaman to corn on the cob,
in today's plain-jane mason jars
quiet, contented yellow kernels
hold super volcanoes, Popocatepetls,

Old Faithful geysers within,
tough layers trapping aggressive steam,
popcorn builds its unbearable pressure
refuses to be constrained,
to split, explode,
burst forth, turn inside out,
pop, pop, pop

into blinding white
snowflakes and mushrooms
and fluffy flowers, fifty times
their original size,
full and freely non-GMO
among slave-trade maize GMO captives
of high fructose corn syrup,
animal feed, processed food,

with popcorn
remaining whole grain victor,
sexy, earthy, savory ancient
of the 21st century.

Lavender Fields Forever

a whiff of lavender stirs up pasts
almost remembered, futures nearly envisioned.

its fragrance you detect right before dreams begin,
what revives you from deepest sleep.

on a sunny day, it's reminiscent of an exotic night.
on a lonely night, reminds you of a much brisker day.

it's early author of the purple
tie-dyed head-trip.

what unknots when you rub its oil behind ears,
on neck's nape, all the way up the temples.

and once inside God's temple,
you long to meld past, present, future.

and so be it, let "lavande" wash your worries,
ease depression, cool a hot headache,

defuse your constant dwelling on deadlines
and schedules, and lead a path to an inescapable

empurpled dwelling place
of perpetual late spring.

Sage, Cedar and Sweetgrass: Sacred Healing Smoke

not in noisy nightclubs
filled with chain smokers
who crack open another pack
of once sacred tobacco.

but outdoors, where smoke
spirals, native rituals begin,
cedar, sage, sweetgrass
wait turns

or together deliver
cleansing swirls
from abalone shell
via turkey feather.

leaders face each
of four directions,
acknowledge four nations,
purify all present of the four colors,

before prayer or sweat lodge,
cup dusty sagebrush smoke
to wash each heart,
thought, flesh,

just as holy water's used
in making the sign of the cross,
excusing ravaged energies
that don't belong.

families who move into houses,
freshly hewn or old-fashioned,
sweep and smudge rooms
with aromatic red cedar smoke.

from kitchens to kids' rooms,

beg cedar's blessings, draw sap-soaked
woods indoors, push what's lingered too long
out yonder.

lastly, sweetgrass,
the first plant to cover native lands?
ember at end of its thick braid
of fragrant plaited hair

forms a thin line of light scent,
using its pale, gentle touch
to lift moods, usher positives,
replace negatives

earlier purged by cedar and sage,
to prepare us now for thanks, prayers,
our ultimate connections,
Ho, Mitakuye Oyasin – all my relations.

Myrrh Images: Fragrant and Medicinal

"The myrrh-like fragrance of Christ is an aroma of life to life to
the repentant and an aroma of death to death to the wicked."
— 2 Corinthians 2:14-16

two myrrhs, three gifts: gold
for kingly Father, frankincense Spirit smoke,
and myrrh, to wrap what's living,
and what passes away.

tree wrapped in skin of gashed bark
as if flogged by Roman soldiers,
open-wound cracks ooze
red-brown resin.

one myrrh, fragrant birth gift,
the other, opiate from pain,
its nuggets crushed
into wine, offered to crucified Christ.

our lips touch what
he wouldn't for our sake;
mix equal parts with honey,
to soothe sore gums like a poultice.

when ready to speak of healing,
sense the duality, present, invisible,
the taking away and the giving,
bitter while pleasing.

Dr. Aloe Vera

generously endowed physician
seated on your windowsill,
mythic green man of fleshly biceps,
waving liquid wands at the sun.

Dr. Aloe Vera of first-aid triage
hidden behind the ficus,
the gel he puckers from his own
broken extremity gives him away.

he shrugs his beefy shoulders at scalds,
oozes compassion that
dries into a bandage,
basks skin in a second one.

sear your hand when you
grabbed the cookie sheet?
Play Ronin with your
razor this morning?

were you sittin' on the
sun-drenched dock of the bay
wasting time...
in your skivvies?

then go to the window,
get close to Dr. Al,
the healer who'll
give his right arm for you,

who'll seal and smooth over
slash and burn with a cool, moistened,
if detached hand,
and nary leave a scar.

Bewitching Witch Hazel

it's a little spooky when the shrub
finally blossoms spider-shaped flowers

around All-Hallows Eve,
after dropping fall leaves.

it's a little spooky when it spits hard,
black seeds like catapults at passersby.

it's a little spooky when lightning storms
turn its clear bottled liquids milky.

but a little bewitching, when at day's end
a woman can face the oval mirror

to let common cotton and witch hazel
usher a balanced beauty, an even complexion,

using this ingenious Halloween trick
to transform ordinary to enchanting

and simultaneously lending air
a hint of autumn apples.

Neem: Pro-Agriculture Ayurvedic

neem, tough Gandhi of a tree,
scratching by on molecules of food,
siphoning shot-glass sips from
the Indian desert.

oily seeds ply non-violent methods
against soybean-eating aphids,
shoo mosquitoes
better than DEET.

neem's quiet insistence persuades
boll weevil, Florida beetle,
mealy bug and locust
to take up fasts.

rather than dine
on the aspirin flavor
and eggy nose
of neem-sprayed leaves.

in passive, non-toxic,
biodegradable resistance
neem does mammals, birds,
bees, earthworms, helpful insects

no harm.

Evening Primrose Path, Rated PG13

unfolding only at day's end,
the evening primrose flower
with dewy jewels on blousy cheeks
steals all attention from the moon.

with one quick night to make seed,
primrose no longer acts prim,
becomes aromatic, her engorged stamens
shimmer like a braless woman in the dark.

working breathy in these chancy, shadowy hours
to attract the right suitors, night-flying moths arrive
to lick petals and raise her cloud of pollen as if
the earth moved, and indeed spill what's fertile fire.

indulged and exhausted, her sepals spread
tangled in dawn's damp bedsheets,
as her seedpod swells, the sweet crevice
from which we draw her fragrant oil,

the oil to replace what
we've lost along our own
non-primrose paths,

which on the plus side
lay as far away as possible
from a flurry of moths.

Comfrey: Banned Herb/Nature's Bandage

knitter, uniter, setter, healer,
triage for the fractured, broken, embattled,
how could comfrey's own reputation be
torn asunder as its one-time advocates pulled apart.

when ancient healers out heal modern ones,
today's med-heads need save face,
point to liver toxicity,
ban herb's internal use.

or would problems arise only
if you drink 20 daily cups of its tea,
or scarf this herb with as much relish
as heart patients' do their burgers and fries?

stronger, sinister pharmaceuticals
find their way onto prescription pads
by means of fine print
no one reads.

in spite of competition,
comfrey salves and ointments proliferate,
down-home growers place its leaves
like bandages over broken ribs,

its homeopathic cousin symphytum
gets a news blackout but orchestrates
personal occupy rallies drawing bone,
cartilage, tissue and skin together as one.

what's been battered and abraded
takes the underground route to the mend,
from the herb that covers its tracks
and leaves little physical evidence behind.

Purple Coneflower Echinacea

every July she arrives for duty,
a sentry in tall cone helmet,
pink petal armor,
oh, decoy of delicacy,
brave flag-bearer blossom.

pretty, popular, powerful
fighter and resister,
each purple-tasseled troop
making lines of defense
against unwanted invaders.

arming us
with abundant arsenals
of roots in our cellars
to help make the common cold
a scarcity.

Feverfew Headache Sandwich

you see zigzags, flashing lights, stars, black holes,
so, you were abducted by a UFO?
chances are, a migraine is about to land
somewhere on the upside of your head.

when sight narrows to tunnel vision,
and your immediate destiny skirts
a white-hot horizon of sub-woofer temple throb,
don't follow this road to its darker destination.

instead, focus on the garden path,
please do eat the daisies, or
better yet, the bitterly fragrant leaves
if the daisy is feverfew.

does your mirror reveal
a face red and flushed?
are you having hot flashes,
but you're a guy?

don't panic, instead, make a sandwich
with feverfew's feathery leaves
between favorite
slices of hearty bread,

then call your workplace,
not to tell them you're calling in sick,
but are indeed coming in,
because your headache's

been abducted
by aliens.

The Ginkgo Tree That Wright Built Next To

sit under Frank Lloyd Wright's ginkgo tree,
think intricate, fan-shaped, striated thoughts,
reconstruct, volley ideas, connect
current culture to collective memory.

but even Wright, unique among thinkers
as this tree is among trees,
couldn't imagine any roof design
to last its same 3,000 years.

contemplate this green, wind-curled canopy,
question whether it offers a youth serum
or homage to what's led up
to this midsummer moment.

is older, or younger better?
does gnarled bark protect from,
or render feeble,
confused rings deep within?

will its pithy strength collapse
under earthquake or avalanche,
or keep buds tender enough to retell Iliad's pains
from first-hand experience?

come autumn, a leaf falls into your lap
like leathery gold,
offers two hemispheres of opinion,
splits the difference.

you absentmindedly hum the tune to
"but you forgot to remember,"
and are no longer the oldest living fossil
in Jurassic Park,

but simply parked under a Jurassic,
wishing boosted concentration
and enhanced recall
on your upcoming test called the rest of your life.

Yucca: Laundering Away Joint Pain

twelve desert yucca dance
waving lush, green headdresses.

deadwood gnarls
across desert floor,

looking like old men's fingers.
rub two bones together,

what do you get?
fired-up joints?

flaming phalanges?
ignited knuckles?

yucca makes its points
over and over

about anti-inflammatory swords foiling
mesa's feverish ways,

while roots and flower bells
whip up laundry tubs of soapweed bubbles,

to cool and cushion
the too close.

Hip Vibe Hawthorn Berry

hip-hop cadence
has nothing on rhythms
of the percussive, tympanic heart,

but if the heart gets into
cacophonous headspace,
thinks too much,

drums with the irregular
rise and fall stock reading
of the straight man,

if it veers from the downbeat
with extra palpitations,
counts messages beyond syncopation

with a throb that's feeble,
too rapid, or with an accent
on the wrong syl-LA-ble,

there's a pattern, a puzzle,
a pulsing, a repeated premise,
variation on a theme,

an endless reprise,
and through hawthorn's
hip synchronization,

without uttering a spoken word,
the heart could groovily bob its head,
continually tap an inspired foot,

if it had either.
its red-blooded, ventricled, auricled self,
thanks to the tom-tom timing of hawthorn,

beats on.

Another Riff on the Licorice Stick

don't hear much about
real licorice sticks anymore,
amidst hot jazz clarinets,
and black candy dished, switched
with understudy star anise.

oh chewable, Scythian root
with more to show
than turning Napoleon's teeth
black,
instead, turns back

the clock when one eats
beyond expiration dates,
curbs drugs' side effects like
the thoughtful pet owner
on a too-narrow sidewalk.

Jonah spent three nights
in a whale's maw,
winding the same path
as pitch-dark licorice that weaves
into your belly's ulcerous depths.

using ebony, sullen shadows
to whip up new stomach cells,
recharge the dome of the abdomen,
to precede dawn's early light
with a more silvery lining.

Milk Thistle Epistle

how do you clean
the cleanser of your
own embodied ecosystem?

to recharge your liver,
which like a bottom feeder,
catfish or oceanic snail,

scours your depths.
what kind of detox spa
can match this janitor's brawn

who filters blood,
vacuums out dross
you toss internally?

was there a sign among the brambles,
when Virgin Mary paused,
nursed baby Jesus,

a drop of her milk falling among thistles,
lending leaves their milky veins,
leaving reminders

of life-sustaining regeneration,
from generation to generation.

Leaf It to Raspberry

torch singer in scarlet sheath,
raspberry "works the womb" to prepare
its female audience to deliver.

men's eyes immediately travel
to raspberry's sweet fruits, but her womanly
secret lies in green leafy curtains behind her.

raspberry's repertoire's versatile,
regulates moon cycles of those who see red,
works through bluesy maladies

and midwifery ways
mixed with nightclub flare,
hopes to write each hopeful

a special script to use when
one's female performance
is both a tough act to live up to

and a hard act to follow.

Stinging Nettle: A Complicated Cupid

nettle's leaves shaped like valentines,
like hearts, bear undersides of love, that sting.

miniature hypodermic needles carry
antidotes to their own upheavals,

fuzzy sharply pointed overtures,
scathe and soothe in one lavish stroke,

to make you unallergic to
whatever you're allergic to.

are you the one attracted, rejected,
seduced, repulsed,

or the other way around?
it's hard to tell between push and pull,

between deep breath and grand exhale,
after which your lungs completely clear.

perhaps you are both the conquered
as well as the cured.

Sleeping with Valerian

stress bunches in clenched fists
like prickly pads of steel wool.
valerian tucks it away in a drawer,

dusts off your palms and
massages them in warm oil,
jumps into bed with you

covers you both with a blanket.

when flu feels like an unrolled blueprint
riddled with specs and explosion call-outs:
scratchy throat, dry lips, skin like hot sand,

parched tongue, cold feet,
valerian folds the noisy document
into a paper airplane and

soars it out your bedroom window.

when insomnia grips at midnight's edge,
he's the parachute you pull that becomes
a curtain letting in the morning.

it's the end of the day, end of the alphabet herb,
the "V" that fast-forwards
through W, X, Y to get to

ZZZZZZs.

but ah yes, his cologne,
a hot hummus of bitter
crushed chrysanthemums

turned sweet, or spoiled honey
laden with
corrupt beeswax,

fermentation of previously fermented.

meanwhile, he banishes
worry, those dishrags
that can't seem to be rung out,

annoyance, repeating bee-buzzing
complaints in your ear, looming deadlines,
stealing second hands from watches and sticking them

into your ankles.

allows you to reach
around either side of your pillow,
grab hold of warm earth with one hand,

lace your fingers through his hair
with the other,
to, at last, soundly and

with complete surrender, sleep.

Vinegar Rebel

we, the ones born,
nurtured, realized,
with hopes to reinvent ourselves
after tasting a flourish of mid-life,
mid-career, mid-malaise sourness.

unlike wine, which can't so closely
coach its progeny – vinegar,
that independent self-inventor,
unwitting unwanted of papa vino
and mother bacteria,
who rebelliously turns even
the best wine so bad,
it might be good.

awakened tangy and sober from inebriated sleep
to recklessly preserve and pickle,
heal and cleanse, deodorize, flavor, soothe,
and set itself stolid survivor
on the cupboard shelf,

after all its intoxicating ancestors
are traded, decanted, toasted and regaled,
with vintages eventually decades out of fashion,
to face barrenness out of the barrel,
unable to replicate themselves to former glories,

the vain fruit of the vine continues, even then,
to disown its offspring vinegar,
rejecting both clear and cloudy,
fluids nonetheless destined to outlive
and outserve their fathers
and every other corked bottle
in the climate-controlled wine cellar.

Dandelion: Weeds Ragged with Riches

after winter snows melt, Tennessee dandelions
raise wild, fringy heads toward the sun,
prompting us to clip, clip,
and sweep them from ours yards.

but dandelions want to sweep us, too,
their bright petals and ragged leaves form
a bottle brush, in a rush to tell us, "It's spring.
Wake up. Time to detox."

golden-capped runways in your lawn
may not be the nuisance you think,
healthier than what's offered in most
grocery store aisles.

teeth of the lion, dandelion green salad,
or sautéed with garlic, pepper flakes, olive oil,
more nutritious than spinach,
and sharper in insight than carrots.

realigning tides of swollen feet, cleansing blood,
clearing skin, bearing up breast milk in new moms,
that imitates juices children squeeze from
dandelions when at play,

and as dandelions say,
"Take all of me, flower, root and leaf,
to enjoy inside your kitchen,
not toss in the compost heap."

Weed Walker

the weed walk guide, Sylvester,
didn't seem happy
to have his hands full
of us for an hour,

hands that would rather be in dirt.
he greeted us kind of ornery,
cranky, his manner unmown
as the weeds close by,

where he began his meander
among odd ragged borders, we trailing
behind formal flower gardens,
neat rows of organic vegetables.

"I prefer Latin names
to the common ones,
weeds have so many designations
juggled in far-flung nations," he said.

"like woody nightshade, bittersweet,
deadly nightshade, belladonna,"
then mumbled ,"it's really solid mom
dulce maria, or something like that!"

Sylvester said he used to
own an herb shop
that went bust,
then turned to selling

oriental rugs,
taking videos of local events
for the chamber,
giving weed tours like this.

he pointed out wild geranium,
geranium robertianum,

"named by some clown Robert,"
he said.

"but most of what I hope to
show youse been weed-whacked.
damn gardeners," he said, but winked.
"weeds being weeds, there's still a plenty. "

he led us to weeds
we 'd eat if hiking or
lost in the woods,
hard up for food,

lamb's quarters from the
amaranth family,
creeping wood-sorrel or
what I called "sour clover" as a kid.

Indian strawberries,
violet flowers, wild alfalfa,
little white carrots
at the roots of queen anne's lace.

on to the weeds that heal,
plaintain or white man's foot,
chew its leaves, place the paste
on a bee sting to relieve pain and itch.

burdock and yellow dock roots,
medicinal for digestion,
gravelroot for kidneys and bladder,
evening primrose for period cramps.

celandine for warts,
snap the stem and apply
its glowing saffron
yellow sap.

finally, poisons,
red baneberry, poison parsnip,

and the aforementioned
deadly nightshade.

"and here's one that's just plain handy,"
he said, "mullein's fuzzy leaves
make great emergency
toilet paper."

these weeds
not so weedy after all,
each with its own personality
and purpose.

so it was with Sylvester,
not named by some clown Sylvester
who named malva sylvestris
or high mallow, but all himself.

not so weedy, a little brambly,
often witty, making the effort
to take us into
his wild, rough-edged world,

the one that borders
what others
consider normal,
of nature's outsiders.

Urban Composter

I slowly spin it like a ferris wheel

our coffee grinds and eggshells,
cucumber peels and avocado skins,
limp celery chunkily chopped,
grass clippings, dried leaves,
dill stalks and parsley stems,
dryer link, corn cobs, paper towels

thrown in to break down in months, even weeks
to waste, rot, unravel and release
a quick legislation that amends and upholds
the backyard garden.

I'm not an alderman, or a mighty alder,
just a worker, a compost carny,
who straps them in as scraps,
lets them sail around a few times,
then bids them "Thank you very mulch"
as they hit the exit ramp
as carbon- and nitrogen-rich soil,
a hot summer joy ride of wetness, corruption and rotation.

in these moments I imitate the earth, that magician
who cracks two eggs into her
top hat and throws the shells
in for good luck,
covers it with the white silk scarf of winter,
then whisks it away
to pull out a bouquet of spring flowers.

the earth revolves,
embraces green, gold, scarlet and brown,
spent plants, cracked rocks, animal waste
and bones of our ancestors,
that fall into its massive arms
to whirl and self-heal,

with leftovers that hold the earth together.

we can only mimic this calling
in teeny, tiny ways with our composters
to feed hungry, postage-stamp gardens
like this one in Chicago,
which swallow compost by the shovelsful
and resurrect it into life-giving, prolific vegetables
with future compost scraps of their own.

Acknowledgments

Many thanks to the publications where poems within *Epicurean Ecstasy* previously appeared:

annapurnamagazine: "Harvesting Goji Berries"

Big Scream: "Beat of the Pumpkin Drum"

Bop Dead City: "Cherries vs. Cherry Blossoms"

Coffee, Tea & Other Beverages anthology: "Green Tea's Ceremony Within"

Drenched chapbook: "Chamomile Earns Its Wings"

Iowa Farmer Today: "Sweet Potatoes: Garnets in the Rough"

Moon Magazine: "Brown Rice Life Coaches," "Massachusetts Cranberries," "Figs: Animal, Vegetable and Mineral?" and "Oats, The Last Grain"

Pirene's Fountain: "May You Have Salty Days Ahead"

Sediment Literary-Arts Journal: "Bewitching Witch Hazel"

Southern Women's Review: "Generations of Beans"

The Broken City: "All-American Blueberries"

The Poet By Day: "Cool Beans"

The Raven's Perch: "Found Champagne in an Unclaimed Wisconsin Corner" and "Vinegar Rebel"

Vitamin ZZZ: "Sleeping with Valerian" and "Lavender Fields Forever"

Wine, Cheese and Chocolate, A Taste of Literary Elegance anthology: "Chocolate and Cocoa: Valentines Crafted 3,000 Years Ago"

Woman Made Gallery Poetry Site: "Multi-taskin' Watermelon"

[. . .]

❁　　❁　　❁

Much appreciation to The Writers' Colony at Dairy Hollow in Eureka Springs, Arkansas, where I was able to put pen to paper on nearly half this book in its Culinary Suite, as well as spend time with further research, revisions and "kitchen-testing." A very special thanks to Steven Foster, leading medicinal plant and herb expert, who took time from his schedule to guide me with research, point out some of the local herbs growing in Arkansas, and treat me as a friend.

And a warm call-out to Bette Pintar, co-explorer during my first herbal field-testing days, with fond memories of discussions spanning countless herbs, formulas and personal experiences, and to my husband Carlos Cumpián, who lovingly encouraged this project. Lastly, to the Marble House Project in Dorset, Vermont, where I shared its lively kitchen with 10 other writing, art, dance and music residents and its organic gardens with fine locals who revealed valuable secrets of both food cultivation and foraging.

Epicurean Ecstasy: More Poems About Food, Drink, Herbs and Spices is the larger sequel to *Omnivore Odes: Poems About Food, Herbs and Spices*, a chapbook of 22 poems which appeared a handful of years ago from Finishing Line Press. Thus, the "More" in *Epicurean Ecstasy*, with all new and a greater number of poems not found in the first volume.

Both poetry books celebrate not only historical and modern pleasures of the kitchen and the table, but also the seasonal evolutions that take place in the cultivated fields and wild terrains, and of those who harvest these foods and bring nourishment to our homes. Both books not only explore, through poetry, the healing properties of a number medicinal herbs and spices, but also the calming and nurturing aspects of some of their aromas, as well as topical and internalized use of their oils and essences. After many years of research and love put into this current offering of poems, I offer a heaping helping of gratitude to The Poetry Box® for finally bringing *Epicurean Ecstasy* to existence as a published full collection.

Praise for *Epicurean Ecstasy*

"Cynthia Gallaher weaves threads of science with seeds of the sacred. The result – a walk along a path that informs with delight. Certainly the best herbal poetry since Shakespeare."

— Steven Foster, senior author of National Geographic's *A Desk Reference of Nature's Medicine* and Peterson's *A Field Guide to Medicinal Plants and Herbs*

"Epicurean Ecstasy: More Poems About Food, Drink, Herbs and Spices is extraordinarily enjoyable; it prompted me to reconsider nourishment and what our own spiritual sustainability requires. Intelligent. Satisfying. Just beautiful. I'm awestruck by Gallaher's dedication in playing a role on insisting on good, healthy food for the community."

— Dee Sweet, Associate Professor Emerita, University of Wisconsin, Green Bay, and Wisconsin State Poet Laureate Emerita

About the Author

Cynthia Gallaher is author of three other full poetry collections: *Earth Elegance*, *Swimmer's Prayer* and *Night Ribbons*, and three poetry chapbooks: *Drenched: Poems About Liquids*; *Omnivore Odes: Poems About Food, Herbs and Spices*; and *Private, On Purpose*.

She also published the nonfiction memoir and reference *Frugal Poets' Guide to Life: How to Live a Poetic Life, Even If You Aren't a Poet*, which won a National Indie Excellence Award.

Gallaher appears on Chicago Public Library's list of "Top Ten Requested Chicago Poets," and was named one of "100 Women Making a Difference" by Today's Chicago Woman magazine for her writing and ecological work. She has also received numerous grants from the City of Chicago Department of Cultural Affairs and the Illinois Arts Council..

Committed to the organic and sustainable foods movement, and a proponent of clean drinking water, Gallaher is a former officer on the board of directors of Illinois Consumers for Safe Food (a local affiliate of The Center for Science in the Public Interest) and has also served as a volunteer for Lake Michigan Federation's (now the Alliance for the Great Lakes) Shorekeepers initiative and the Green Team of the Chicago Park District. She is also a certified yoga instructor and aromatherapist.

About The Poetry Box®

The Poetry Box® was founded by Shawn Aveningo Sanders & Robert R. Sanders, who wholeheartedly believe that every day spent with the people you love, doing what you love, is a moment in life worth cherishing. Their boutique press celebrates the talents of their fellow artisans and writers through professional book design and publishing of individual collections, as well as their flagship literary journal, *The Poeming Pigeon*.

Feel free to visit the online bookstore (thePoetryBox.com), where you'll find more titles including:

Keeping It Weird: Poems & Stories of Portland, Oregon

The Way a Woman Knows by Carolyn Martin

Giving Ground by Lynn M. Knapp

Broadfork Farm by Tricia Knoll

Psyche's Scroll by Karla Linn Merrifield

Painting the Heart Open by Liz Nakazawa

Fireweed by Gudrun Bortman

14: Antologia del Sonoran by Christopher Bogart

November Quilt by Penelope Scambly Schott

My Life in Cars by Linda Strevers

Shrinking Bones by Judy K. Mosher

Many Sparrows by donnarkevic

and more . . .

CPSIA information can be obtained
at www.ICGtesting.com
Printed in the USA
FFHW010013141118
49357659-53636FF